piano • vocal • guitar

favorite hymns

Hal Leonard Publishing Corporation

7777 West Bluemound Road P.O. Box 13819 Milwaukee, WI 53213

ISBN 0-7935-0062-1

ABIDE WITH ME

Words by HENRY F. LYTE
Music by WILLIAM H. MONK

ALL HAIL THE POWER OF JESUS' NAME!

Words by E. PERRONET
Music by OLIVER HOLDEN

All hail the power of Je - sus' name. Let an - gels pros - trate

fall. Bring forth the roy - al di - a - dem and

crown   Him   Lord   of _____ all.   Bring

forth   the   roy - al   di - a - dem   and   crown   Him

Lord _____ of   all.   Let

2. Let ev'ry kindred, ev'ry tribe on this terrestrial ball.
   To Him all majesty ascribe and crown Him Lord of all.
   To Him all majesty ascribe and crown Him Lord of all.

3. Oh, that with yonder sacred throng we at his feet may fall.
   We'll join the everlasting song and crown Him Lord of all.
   We'll join the everlasting song and crown Him Lord of all.

ALL PEOPLE THAT ON EARTH DO DWELL

Additional Lyrics

2. Know that the Lord is God indeed:
   Without our aid He did us make;
   We are His folk, He doth us feed,
   And for His sheep He doth us take.

3. O enter then His gates with praise,
   Approach with joy His courts unto;
   Praise, laud, and bless His name always,
   For it is seemly so to do.

4. For why? The Lord God is good.
   His mercy is forever sure;
   His truth at all times firmly stood,
   and shall from age to age endure. Amen.

ALL THINGS BRIGHT AND BEAUTIFUL

AMAZING GRACE

Verse 3
And when this flesh and heart shall fail
and mortal life shall cease.
I shall possess within the veil
a life of joy and peace.

When we've been there ten thousand years,
bright shining as the sun.

We've no less days to sing God's praise
than when we first begun.

AVE MARIA

Music by FRANZ SCHUBERT
Traditional liturgical text

Very slowly

*pronounced grah - tsee - ah

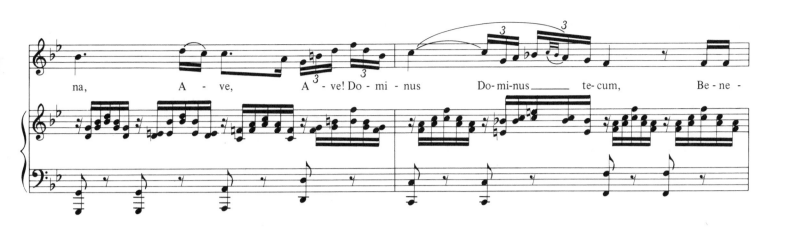

na, A - ve, A - ve! Do - mi - nus Do - mi - nus_____ te - cum, Be - ne -

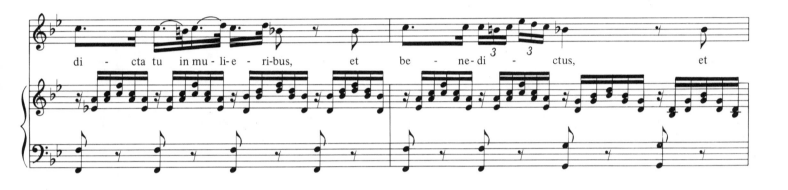

di - cta tu in mu - li - e - ri - bus, et be - ne - di - ctus, et

be - ne - di - ctus fru - ctus ven - tris, ven - tris, tu - i, Je - sus.**

fp *pp*

A - ve Ma - ri - a!

** pronounced yeh - zoos

ho - ra mor - tis no - strae, in ho - ra mor - tis, mor - tis no - strae, in

ho - ra mor - tis no - strae. A - ve Ma - ri

D.S. al Coda

a!

CODA

dim.

BE STILL, MY SOUL

Original Text by KATHARINA VON SCHLEGEL
This Translation by JANE L. BORTHWICK
Music by JEAN SIBELIUS

3. Be still, my soul; the hour is hast'ning on
When we shall be forever with the Lord,
When disappointment, grief, and fear are gone.

Sorrow forgot, love's purest joys restored.
Be still, my soul; when change and tears are past,
All safe and blessed we shall meet at last.

BEAUTIFUL ISLE OF SOMEWHERE

Words by JESSIE BROWN POUNDS
Music by JOHN S. FEARIS

BLESSED ASSURANCE

Words by F.J. CROSBY
Music by Mrs. JOS. F. KNAPP

BLEST BE THE TIE THAT BINDS

H.G. NAGELI

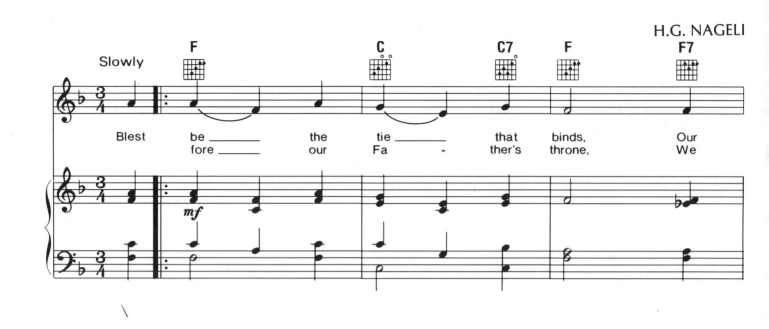

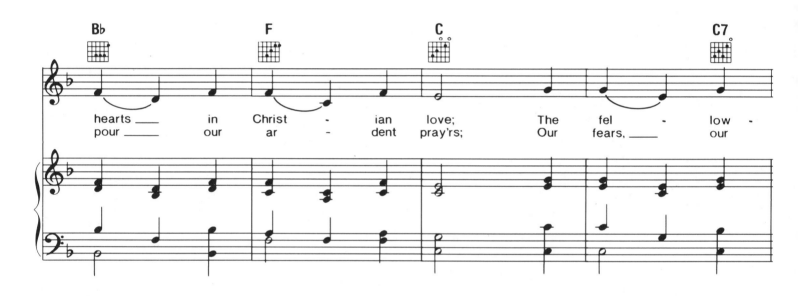

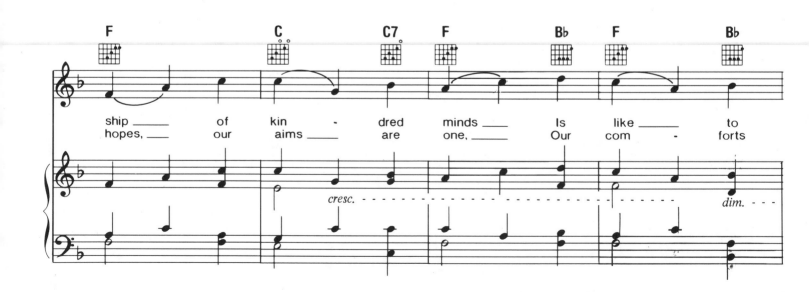

BRINGING IN THE SHEAVES

Words by KNOWLES SHAW
Music by GEORGES MINOR

3. Going forth with weeping, sowing for the Master.
Tho' the loss sustained our spirit often grieves;
When our weeping's over, He will bid us welcome,
We shall come rejoicing, bringing in the sheaves.

CHRIST THE LORD IS RISEN TODAY

Words and Music by CHARLES WESLEY

2. Lives again our glorious King: Alleluia!
   Where, O death, is now thy sting? Alleluia!
   Dying once, He all doth save: Alleluia!
   Where thy victory, O grave? Alleluia!

3. Love's redeeming work is done, Alleluia!
   Fought the fight, the battle won: Alleluia!
   Death in vain forbids Him rise: Alleluia!
   Christ has opened Paradise. Alleluia!

4. Soar we now, where Christ has led, Alleluia!
   Foll'wing our exalted Head: Alleluia!
   Made like Him, like Him we rise: Alleluia!
   Ours the cross, the grave, the skies. Alleluia!

THE CHURCH IN THE WILDWOOD

WILLIAM S. PITTS

With Movement

There's a church in the val-ley by the wild-wood, No love-li-er spot in the dale; No-

place is so dear to my child-hood As the lit-tle brown church in the vale.

Come to The Church In The Wild-wood, Oh, come to the church in the vale! No—

2. O come to the church in the wildwood,
To the trees where the wild flowers bloom;
Where the parting hymn will be changed,
We will weep by the side of the tomb.

3. From the church in the valley by the wildwood,
When day fades away into night,
I would fain from this spot of my childhood,
Wing my way to the mansions of light.

COME, THOU ALMIGHTY KING

With An Easy Flow

FELICE GIARDINI

3. Come, holy Comforter!
   Thy sacred witness bear,
   In this glad hour:
   Thou who almighty art,
   Now rule in ev'ry heart,
   And ne'er from us depart,
   Spirit of pow'r!

4. To the great One in Three,
   The highest praises be,
   Hence ever more!
   His sov'reign majesty
   May we in glory see,
   And to eternity
   Love and adore.

THE CHURCH'S ONE FOUNDATION

Words by SAMUEL J. STONE
Music by SAMUEL S. WESLEY

2. Elect from every nation,
   Yet one o'er all the earth,
   Her charter of salvation,
   One Lord, one faith, one birth;
   One holy name she blesses,
   Partakes one holy food,
   And to one hope she presses,
   With every grace endued.

3. 'Mid toil and tribulation,
   And tumult of her war,
   She waits the consummation
   Of peace for evermore;
   Till with the vision glorious,
   Her longing eyes are blest,
   And the great Church victorious
   Shall be the Church at rest.

4. Yet she on earth hath union
   With God, the Three in One,
   And mystic sweet communion
   With those whose rest is won;
   O happy ones and holy!
   Lord give us grace that we
   Like them, the meek and lowly,
   On high may dwell with Thee.

CLEANSE ME

Words by EDWIN ORR
Music by V.O. FOSSETT

2. I praise Thee, Lord, for cleansing me of sin.
   Fulfill Thy Word and make me pure within.
   Fill me with fire where once I burned with shame.
   Grant my desire to magnify Thy Name.

3. Lord, take my life and make it wholly Thine.
   Fill my poor heart with Thy great love devine.
   Take all my will, my passion, self, and pride.
   I now surrender, Lord, in me abide.

4. O Holy Ghost, revival comes from Thee.
   Send a revival, start the work in me.
   Thy Word declares Thou wilt supply our need.
   For blessing now, O Lord, I humbly plead.

CROWN HIM WITH MANY CROWNS

M. BRIDGES

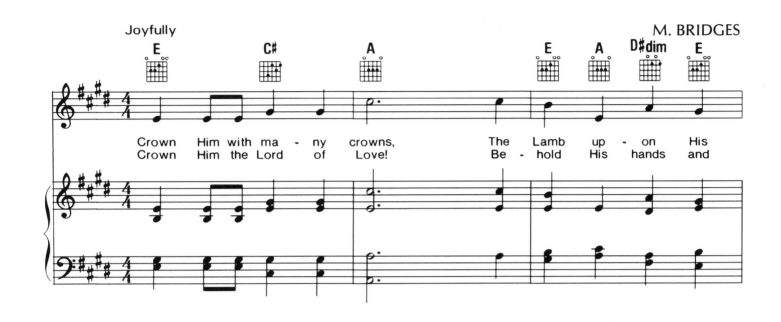

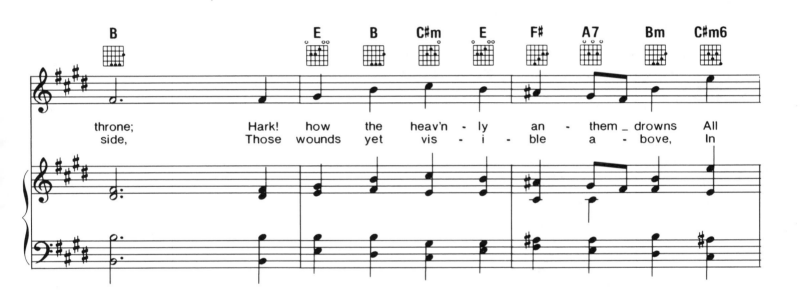

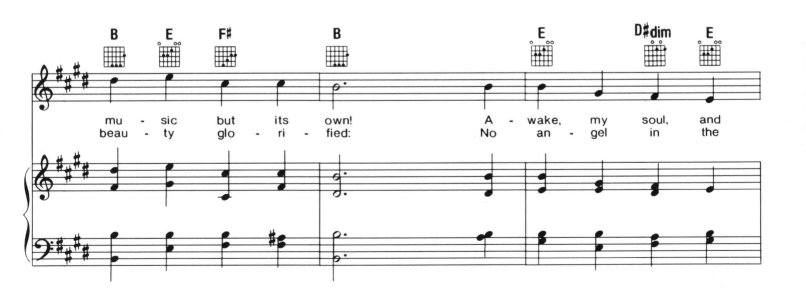

3. Crown Him the Lord of life, Who triumphed o'er the grave
   And rose victorious in the strife for those He came to save.
   His glories now we sing, Who dies and rose on high,
   Who dies eternal life to bring and lives that death may die.

FAIREST LORD JESUS
(CRUSADER'S HYMN)

C.E. HAUPT

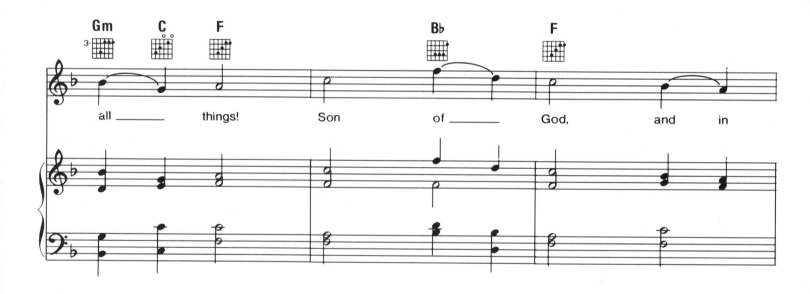

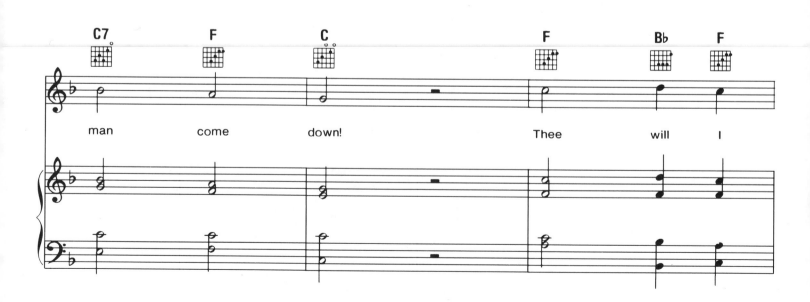

love _____ and Thee will I hon - or:

Thou art my soul's bright Joy and Crown.

2. Fair are the forests, yet more fair the green fields
In the springtime's beauteous day:
Jesus is fairer, Jesus is truer,
'Tis He our sorrowing hearts makes gay.

3. Bright shines the moonbeam, yet more bright the sungleam,
And in heav'n each twinkling star:
Jesus shines fairer, Jesus shines truer,
Than all the hosts of Angels are.

4. Fairest Lord Jesus! Ruler of all nature!
O Thou of God and man the Son!
Thee will I honor,
Thee Will I cherish,
Thou my soul's glory, joy, and crown.

5. Fair are the meadows, Fairer still the woodlands,
Robed in the blooming garb of spring;
Jesus is fairer, Jesus is purer,
Who makes the woeful heart to sing.

6. Fair is the sunshine, Fairer still the moonlight,
And all the twinkling starry host;
Jesus shines brighter, Jesus shines purer,
Than all the angels heav'n can boast!

FAITH OF OUR FATHERS

Adapted by WILLIS RAY

Faith of our fa - thers! liv - ing still
Our fa - thers, chained __ in pris - ons dark,
Faith of our fa - thers! we __ will love

In spite of dun - geon, fire, __ and sword,
Were still in heart and con - science free;
Both friend and foe in all __ our strife,

FOR THE BEAUTY OF THE EARTH

* for Holy Communion

GIVE ME THAT OLD TIME RELIGION

3. It was good for old Abe Lincoln;
It was good for old Abe Lincoln.
It was good for old Abe Lincoln,
And it's good enough for me.

GOD OF OUR FATHERS

HE'S GOT THE WHOLE WORLD IN HIS HANDS

HIS EYE IS ON THE SPARROW

Words by CIVILLA D. MARTIN
Music by CHARLES H. GABRIEL

HOLY GOD, WE PRAISE THY NAME

Words by CLARENCE WALWORTH
Music from an old Austrian Hymnal

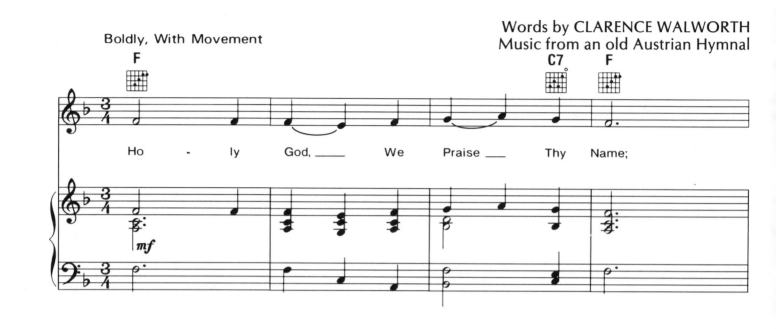

Ho - ly God, ____ We Praise ____ Thy Name;

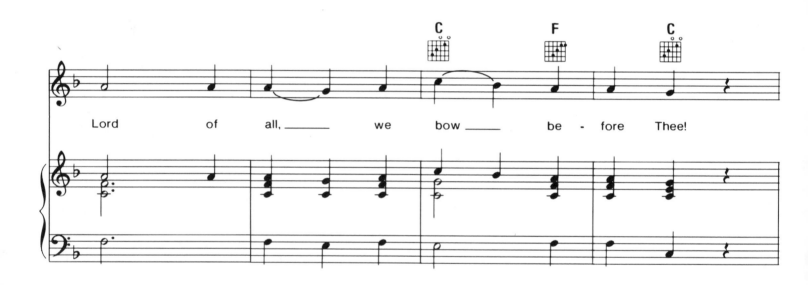

Lord of all, ____ we bow ____ be - fore Thee!

All on earth ____ Thy scep - tre claim, All in

HOLY, HOLY, HOLY

Words by REGINALD HEBER
Music by J.B. DYKES

HOW SWEET THE NAME OF JESUS SOUNDS

Words by JOHN NEWTON
Music by ALEXANDER RAINAGLE

I KNOW THAT MY REDEEMER LIVES

Words by SAMUEL MEDLEY
Music by JOHN HATTON

I LOVE THY KINGDOM, LORD

A.B. EVERETT

Moderately Slow

I Love Thy King - dom, _ Lord, The _ house of _ Thine a -

bode; The Church our blest Re - deem - er ___ saved with

His own _ pre - cious blood. I love Thy Church, O ____

I LOVE TO TELL THE STORY

IN THE GARDEN

IN THE SWEET BY AND BY

way ... to pre-pare us a dwell-ing place there.
more, ... not a sigh for the bless-ing of rest.
love ... and the bless-ings that hal-low our days.

In the sweet ... by and by, ... we shall meet on that beau-ti-ful

shore. ... In the sweet ... by and by ... we shall

meet on that beau-ti-ful shore. ... We shall
To our shore.

I SURRENDER ALL

Words by JUDSON VAN DeVENTER
Music by WINFIELD WEEDEN

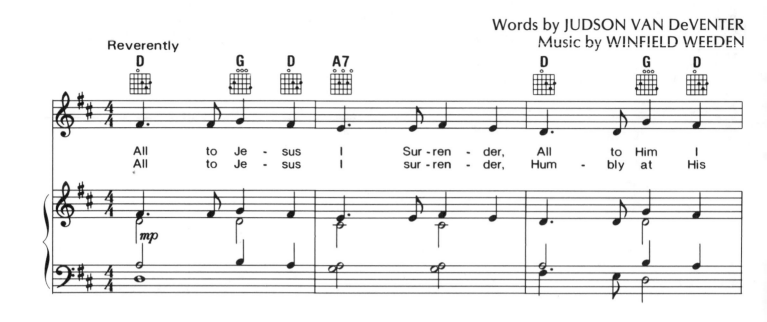

All to Je - sus I Sur - ren - der, All to Him I
All to Je - sus I sur - ren - der, Hum - bly at His

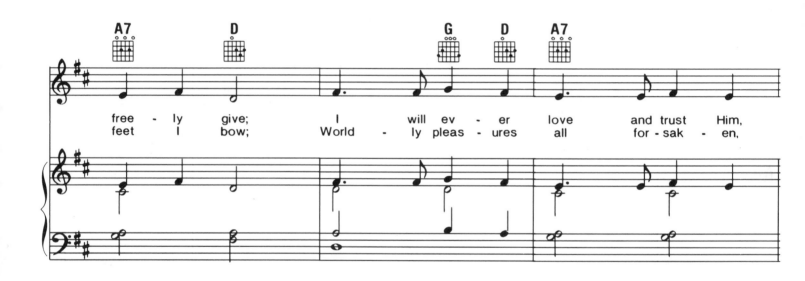

free - ly give; I will ev - er love and trust Him,
feet I bow; World - ly pleas - ures all for - sak - en,

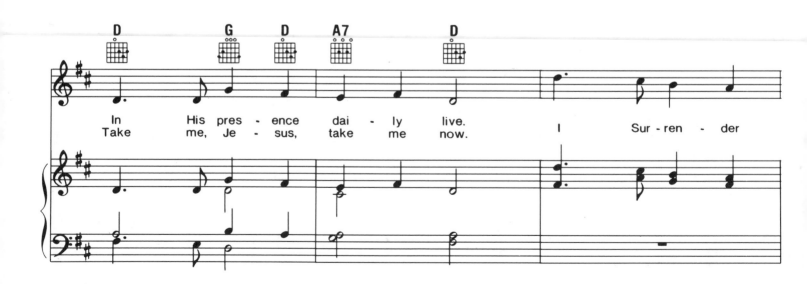

In His pres - ence dai - ly live. I Sur - ren - der
Take me, Je - sus, take me now.

3. All to Jesus I surrender,
   Make me, Savior, wholly Thine;
   Let me feel the Holy Spirit,
   Truly know that Thou art mine.

4. All to Jesus I surrender,
   Lord, I give myself to Thee;
   Fill me with Thy love and power,
   Let Thy blessing fall on me.

JESUS, SAVIOR, PILOT ME

JESUS CHRIST IS RISEN TODAY

JESUS LOVES ME!

Words by ANNA WARNER
Music by WILLIAM BRADBURY

JESUS, LOVER OF MY SOUL

S.B. MARSH

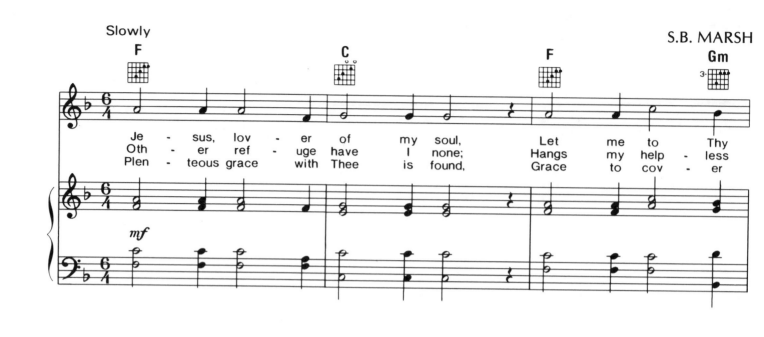

JOYFUL, JOYFUL WE ADORE THEE

JUST A CLOSER WALK WITH THEE

JUST AS I AM

W.B. BRADBURY

Slowly, with movement

KUM BA YAH

From Angola Africa

Kum ba yah, my Lord, Kum ba yah! Kum ba yah, my Lord, Kum ba
cry - in', Lord, Kum ba yah! Some - one's cry - in', Lord, Kum ba

yah! Kum ba yah, my Lord, Kum ba yah! O Lord, __ Kum ba
yah! Some - one's cry - in', Lord, Kum ba yah! O Lord, __ Kum ba

yah! Some - one's yah! Hmm __

LO, HOW A ROSE E'ER BLOOMING

By MICHAEL PRAETORIUS

THE LORD BLESS YOU AND KEEP YOU

LEANING ON THE EVERLASTING ARMS

Words by ELISHA HOFFMAN
Music by ANTHONY SHOWALTER

Confidently

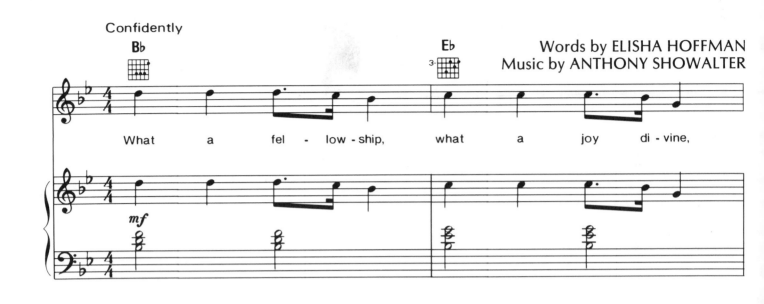

What a fel - low - ship, what a joy di - vine,

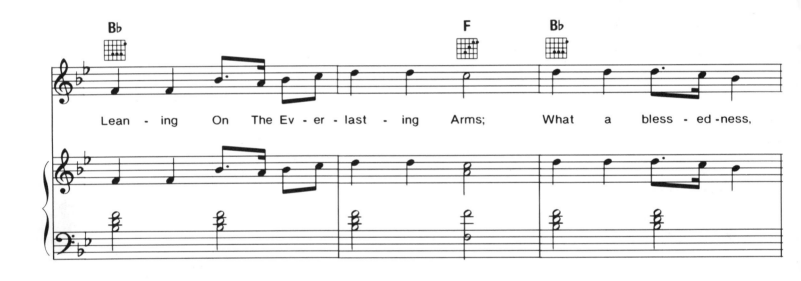

Lean - ing On The Ev - er - last - ing Arms; What a bless - ed - ness,

what a peace is mine, Lean - ing On The Ev - er - last - ing Arms.

NOBODY KNOWS THE TROUBLE I SEE

A MIGHTY FORTRESS IS OUR GOD

Words and Music by MARTIN LUTHER

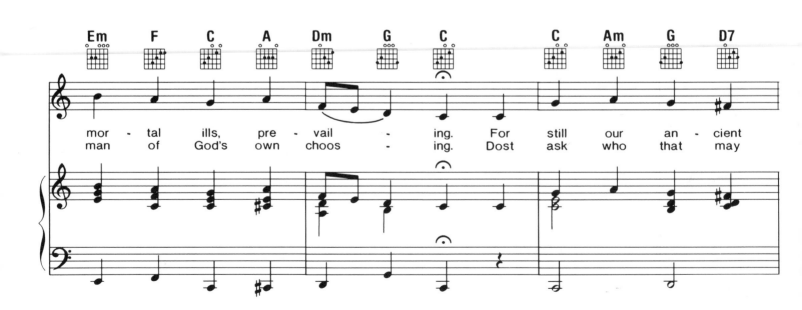

3. And tho this world, with devils filled,
Should threaten to undo us;
We will not fear, for God hath willed
His truth to triumph through us;
The Prince of darkness grim,
We tremble not for him;
His rage we can endure,
For lo! His doom is sure,
One little word shall fell him.

4. That word above all earthly powers,
No thanks to them abideth,
The spirit and the gifts are ours
Through Him who with us sideth;
Let goods and kindred go,
This mortal life also;
The body they may kill;
God's truth abideth still,
His kingdom is forever.

NEARER, MY GOD, TO THEE

Moderately

Near - er, my God, to Thee, near - er to
Tho' like the wan - der - er The sun to gone

Thee! E'en though it be a cross
down, Dark - ness be o - ver me

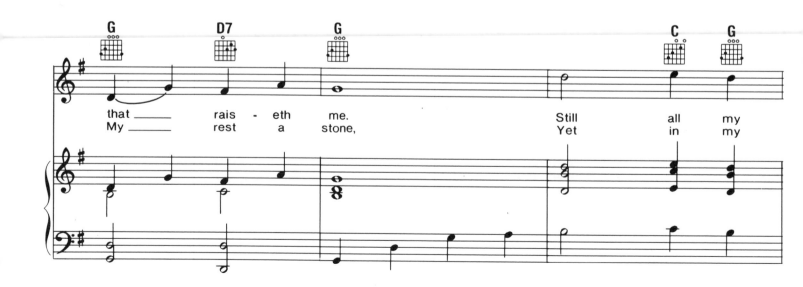

that ___ rais - eth me. Still all my
My ___ rest a stone, Yet in my

3. Then with my waking tho'ts
Bright with Thy praise,
Out of my stony griefs
Bethel I'll raise
So by my woes to be,
Nearer, my God, to Thee,
Nearer, my God, to Thee,
Nearer to Thee!

4. Or if on joyful wing,
Cleaving the sky,
Sun, moon, and stars forgot,
Upwards I'll fly,
Still all my song shall be,
Nearer, my God, to Thee,
Nearer, my God, to Thee,
Nearer to Thee!

NOW THANK WE ALL OUR GOD

Words by MARTIN RINKART
Music by JOHANN CRUGAR

blessed us on our way With count - less gifts of
love, And still is ours to - day. O more.

2. (O) may this bounteous God
   Through all our life be near us,
   With ever joyful hearts
   And blessed peace to cheer us;
   And keep us in His grace,
   And guide us when perplexed,
   And free us from all ills,
   In this world and the next.

3. (All) praise and thanks to God
   The Father now be given,
   The Son and Him who reigns
   With them in highest heaven;
   The one eternal God,
   Whom earth and heav'n adore;
   For thus it was, is now,
   And shall be evermore.

NOW THE DAY IS OVER

O GOD, OUR HELP IN AGES PAST

O SACRED HEAD, NOW WOUNDED

THE OLD RUGGED CROSS

ONLY TRUST HIM

JOHN STOCKTON

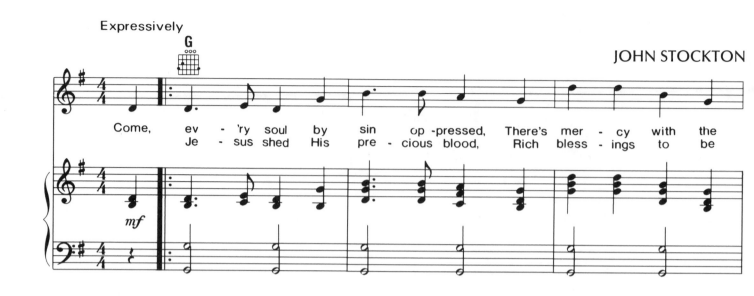

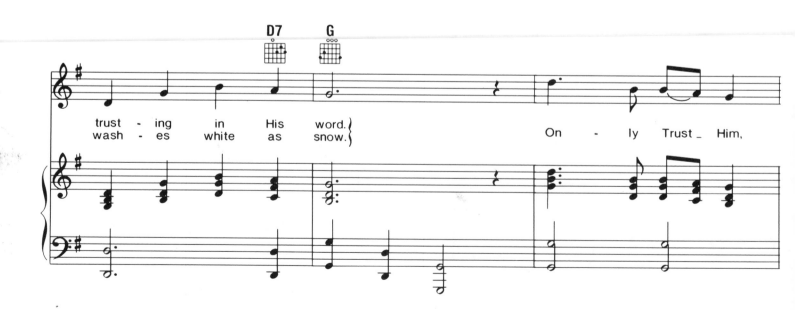

3. Yes, Jesus is the truth, the way,
   That leads you into rest;
   Believe in Him without delay,
   And you are fully blest.

4. Come, then, and join this holy band,
   And on to glory go,
   To dwell in that celestial land,
   Where joys immortal flow.

ONWARD CHRISTIAN SOLDIERS

By Sir ARTHUR SULLIVAN
and SABINE BARINE-GOULD

March Tempo

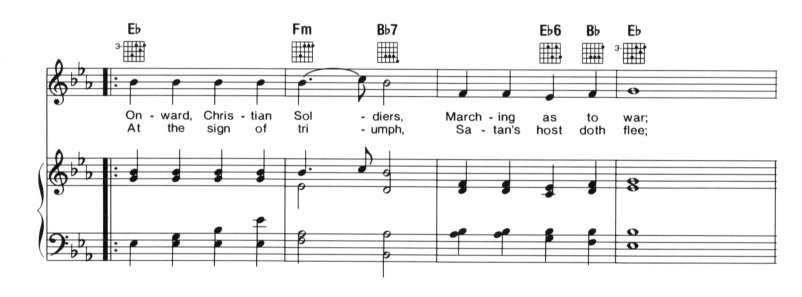

On - ward, Chris - tian Sol - diers, March - ing as to war;
At the sign of tri - umph, Sa - tan's host doth flee;

With the cross of Je - sus Go - ing on be - fore.
On then, Chris - tian sol - diers, On to vic - to - ry.

131

PRAISE TO THE LORD, THE ALMIGHTY

Words by CATHERINE WINKWORTH
Music from "Praxis Pietatis Melica"

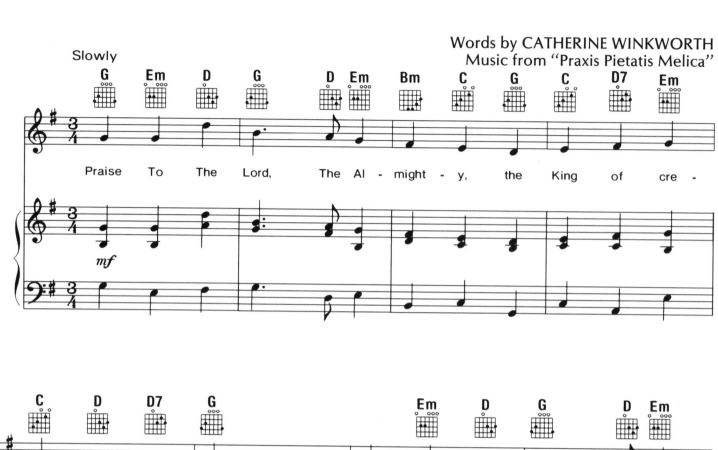

Praise To The Lord, The Al - might - y, the King of cre -

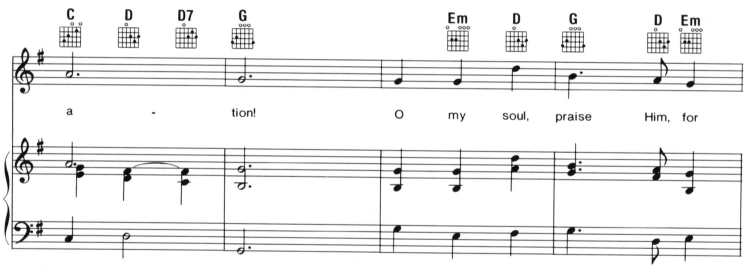

a - tion! O my soul, praise Him, for

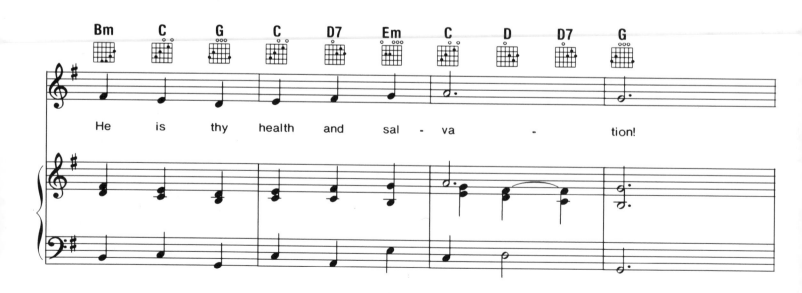

He is thy health and sal - va - tion!

PRAISE MY SOUL
THE KING OF HEAVEN

PRECIOUS MEMORIES

3. As I travel on life's pathway, I know not what life shall hold;
   As I wander hopes grow fonder, Precious mem'ries flood my soul.

REVIVE US AGAIN

Words by WILLIAM MACKAY
Music by JOHN HUSBAND

ROCK OF AGES

3. While I draw this fleeting breath,
When my eyes shall close in death,
When I rise to worlds unknown,
And behold Thee on Thy throne,
Rock Of Ages cleft for me,
Let me hide myself in Thee.

SAVIOR, LIKE A SHEPHERD LEAD US

Words by DOROTHY THRUPP
Music by WILLIAM BRADBURY

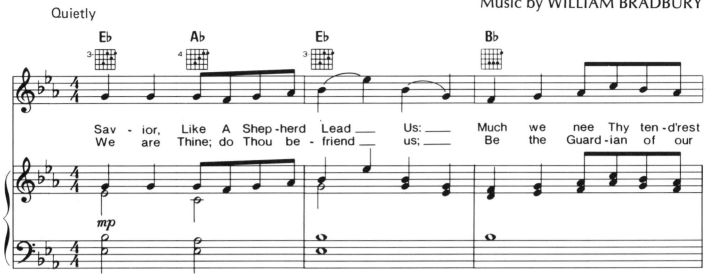

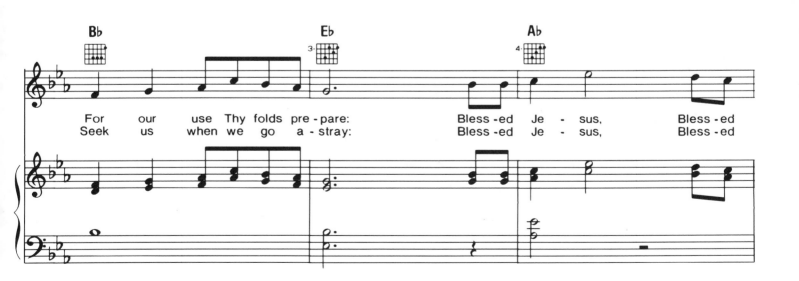

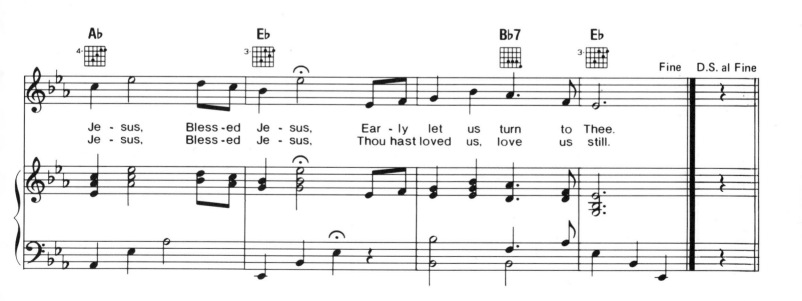

SHALL WE GATHER AT THE RIVER?

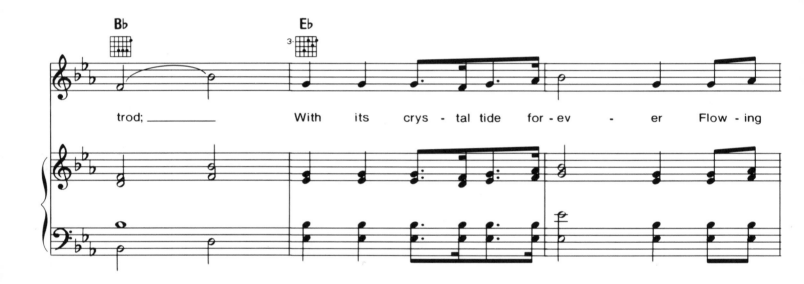

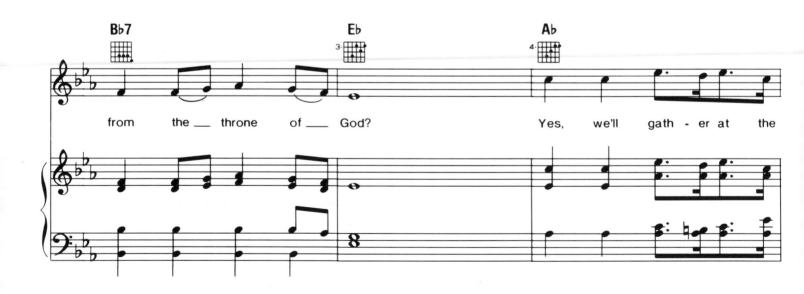

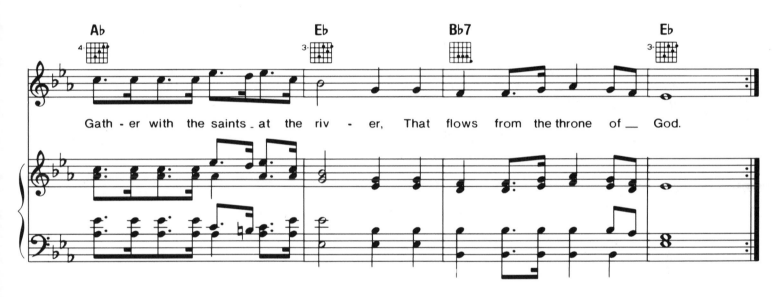

2. On the margin of the river,
   Washing up its silver spray,
   We shall walk and worship ever
   All the happy, golden day.

3. On the bosom of the river,
   Where the Saviour King we own,
   We shall meet and sorrow never
   'Neath the glory of the throne.

4. Ere we reach the shining river,
   Lay we ev'ry burden down:
   Grace our spirits will deliver,
   And provide a robe and crown.

5. Soon we'll reach the shining river,
   Soon our pilgrimage will cease;
   Soon our happy hearts will quiver
   With the melody of peace.

SOFTLY AND TENDERLY JESUS IS CALLING

Words and Music by WILL L. THOMPSON

Moderately Slow

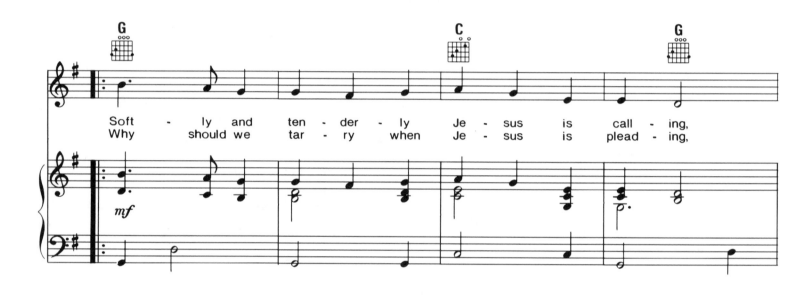

Soft - ly and ten - der - ly Je - sus is call - ing,
Why should we tar - ry when Je - sus is plead - ing,

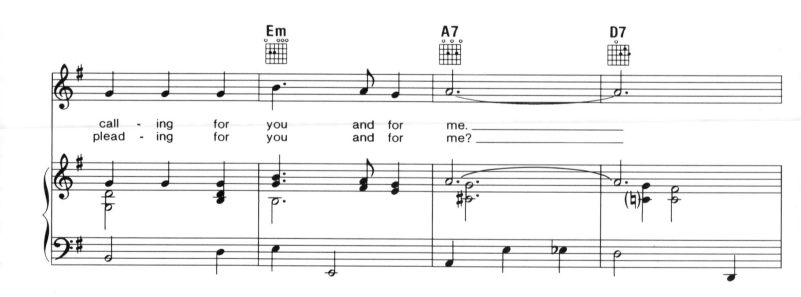

call - ing for you and for me.
plead - ing for you and for me?

151

STAND UP! STAND UP FOR JESUS

Words and Music by GEORGE DUFFIELD
and GEORGE J. WEBB

2. Stand up, stand up for Jesus,
   The strife will not be long;
   This day the noise of battle,
   The next, the victor's song;
   To him the overcometh,
   A crown of life shall be;
   He with the King of glory
   Shall reign eternally.

SWEET HOUR OF PRAYER

Words by WILLIAM W. WALFORD
Music by WILLIAM B. BRADBURY

Moderately

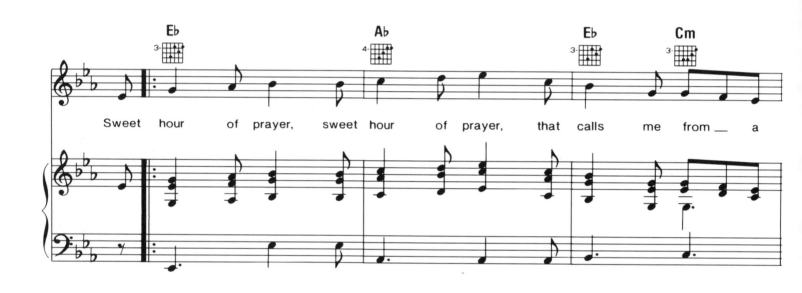

Sweet hour of prayer, sweet hour of prayer, that calls me from __ a

world of care And bids me at my Fa - ther's throne: Make all my wants and

2. (Sweet) hour of prayer,
Sweet hour of prayer,
thy wings shall my petition bear
To Him whose truth and faithfulness
engage the waiting soul to bless.
And since He bids me seek His face,
believe His word, and trust His grace,
I'll cast on Him my ev-'ry care
and wait for thee, sweet hour of prayer.

3. (Sweet) hour of prayer,
sweet hour of prayer,
may I thy consolation share
Till from Mount Pisgah's lofty height
I view my home and take my flight.
This robe of flesh I'll drop and rise
to seize the everlasting prize
And shout while passing through the air
farewell, farewell, sweet hour of prayer.

SWING LOW, SWEET CHARIOT

Spiritual

THIS IS MY FATHER'S WORLD

Words by MALTBIE BABCOCK
Traditional English Melody

THE WAYFARING STRANGER

Spiritual

I am a poor _____ way-far-ing stran-ger, while trav'-ling
clouds _____ will ga-ther round me, I know my

through _____ this world of woe, Yet there's no sick - ness, toil nor
way _____ is rough and steep; But gol-den fields _____ lie out be-

dan-ger in that bright world _____ to which I go. I'm go-ing
fore me where God's re-deemed _____ shall ev-er sleep. I'm go-ing

164

WHAT A FRIEND WE HAVE IN JESUS

Words by JOSEPH SCRIVEN
Music by C.C. CONVERSE

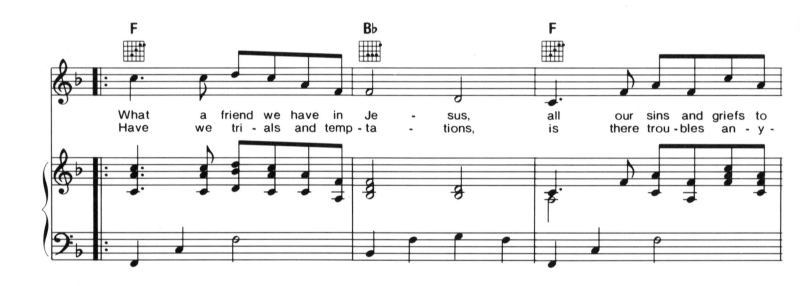

What a friend we have in Je - sus, all our sins and griefs to
Have we tri - als and temp - ta - tions, is there trou - bles an - y -

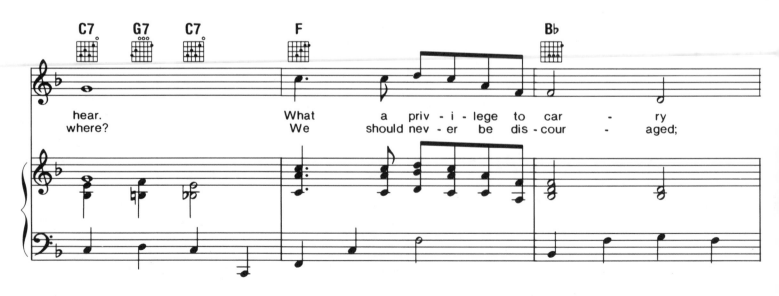

hear. What a priv - i - lege to car - ry
where? We should nev - er be dis - cour - aged;

3. Are we weak and heavy laden,
cumbered with a load of care?
Precious Savior still our refuge;
take it to the Lord in prayer.
Do thy friends despise, forsake thee?
Take it to the Lord in prayer.
In His arms He'll take and shield thee;
thou will find a solace there.

WHEN I SURVEY THE WONDROUS CROSS

Words by ISAAC WATTS
Music by LOWELL MASON

Moderately

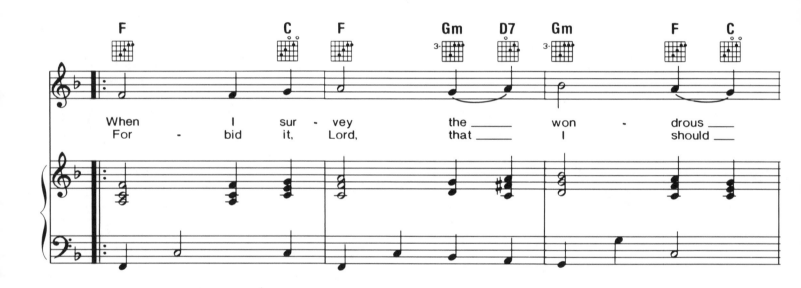

When I sur - vey the won - drous
For - bid it, Lord, that I should

cross On which the Prince of
boast Save in the death of

3. See, from His head, His hands, His feet,
Sorrow and love flow mingled down
Did e'er such love and sorrow meet
Or thorns compose so rich a crown.

4. Were the whole realm of nature mine,
That were a present far too small.
Love so amazing so divine,
Demands my soul, my life, my all.

WHISPERING HOPE

Soft as the voice of an an -
If in the dusk of an the twi -

gel, breath - ing a les - son un -
light, dim be the re - gion a -

heard. Hope with a
far. Will not the

WERE YOU THERE?

Spiritual

Moderately

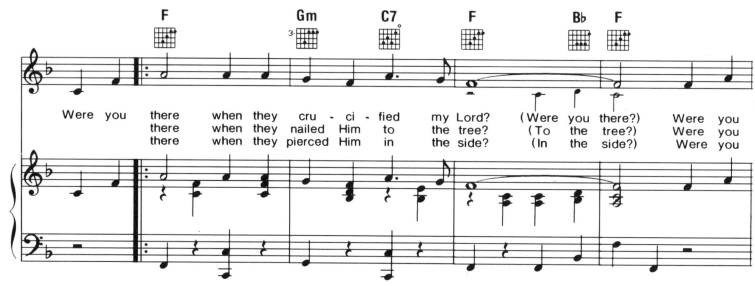

Were you there when they cru-ci-fied my Lord? (Were you there?) Were you
there when they nailed Him to the tree? (To the tree?) Were you
there when they pierced Him in the side? (In the side?) Were you

there when they cru-ci-fied my Lord? _____ Oh, _____
there when they nailed Him to the tree? _____ Oh, _____
there when they pierced Him in the side? _____ Oh, _____